the little *bit naughty* book of

# sex

## positions

the little *bit naughty* book of

# sex

## positions

Siobhan Kelly

Amorata Press

Published in the U.S. by
Amorata Press,
an imprint of Ulysses Press
P.O. Box 3440
Berkeley, CA 94703
www.amoratapress.com

10 9 8 7 6 5 4 3

First published as *The Ann Summers Book of Red Hot Positions* in 2005 by Ebury Press
Random House, 20 Vauxhall Bridge Road, London SW1V 2SA

Library of Congress Control Number 2004110288
ISBN 1-56975-450-0

Art direction and design by Smith & Gilmour, London
Make-up by Bettina Graham
Photography by John Freeman

Printed and bound in Singapore by Tien Wah Press

Distributed by Publishers Group West

# contents

Welcome to **The Little Bit Naughty Book of Sex Positions**. This follows our very successful **The Little Bit Naughty Book of Sex** which literally flew off the shelves! Since we couldn't fit it all into the last book we decided to bring you more sex tips with this book. We hope that by reading this book we will help you spice up your sex life. If you are looking for new ideas then we have them all! Don't be afraid to experiment! Remember, a healthy sex life is vital for maintaining a healthy relationship. Have fun!

# woman on top

Girl power! Sex is adventurous and orgasmic when women take the lead in bed. These positions are great for women who like to be in control – and he'll love it when you show off your body and let him lie back and relax for a change.

# reverse rodeo

**HOW TO DO IT** He lies back and she squats over him, facing his feet, and slowly lowers herself onto his erection. She leans on her hands and bounces up and down or, if she wants to show off how flexible she is, she can lean back over his chest so that they are lying cheek-to-cheek.

**WHAT'S RIGHT WITH IT?** There's not much work in here for the man. When she's sitting up, he's free to stimulate her anus and perineum if that's what she likes; and if she's lying back, he can reach her clitoris. Because you can't see each other, you're free to let your fantasies run wild. It's the only way to combine the thrill of rear-entry sex with the snug fit of woman-on-top sex.

**WHAT'S WRONG WITH IT?** It can take a while to find a position with which both partners are comfortable and offers little clitoral stimulation for her through intercourse alone; unless she lies back he can't reach her clitoris, so she'll have to stimulate it herself.

**VARIATIONS ON THE THEME** She could start by sitting on his face to give her arousal a head start and then work her way down his body.

**HOW TO DO IT** He lies on his back; he may find it more comfortable with his head propped up on pillows or resting in his cradled hands. She straddles him and gently slides herself down onto his erection and uses her thighs to move up and down.

**WHAT'S RIGHT WITH IT?** It's great for the guy because all he has to do is lie back and enjoy the experience – watching her breasts bounce up and down is a huge visual treat for him. Both partners have access to her breasts and clitoris and he can use his hands to guide her hips into the rhythm he likes. This is a great position during pregnancy as her 'bump' won't be squashed.

**WHAT'S WRONG WITH IT?** Unless she has the thighs of a horse-riding champion, this position can get very tiring very quickly, and can induce cramp. What's more, some women say that it makes them feel too exposed. The position can be frustrating for the man who likes to control the thrusting during sex, although he can grab hold of her buttocks or her waist to help her move up and down.

**VARIATIONS ON THE THEME** This is a great opportunity to wear sexy lingerie or to show off a fantasy outfit during sex: why not try a chiffon and marabou nightie or a see-through negligée?

**HOW TO DO IT** He lies back on pillows with his legs apart, while she lowers herself onto his penis and slowly, slowly, shifts back until she's lying backwards at a similar angle to him, with her legs extended. From the side, the two of you should look like the letter X.

**WHAT'S RIGHT WITH IT?** You've got great eye contact and can see the penis sliding in and out of the vagina, which is a big turn-on. Penetration feels unusual, especially at the tip of his dick, and because there's little range of movement, the man's orgasm can be delayed. This is great if either of you is particularly heavy or become claustrophobic during body-contact sex – you both have a real sense of your own space as you're joined at the hip and nowhere else.

**WHAT'S WRONG WITH IT?** Gently does it with this position: the penis is at an unusual and precarious angle. Pull out too quickly and you'll know about it for the wrong reasons. Because of the delicate nature of the position, you're going to have to take it slow.

**VARIATIONS ON THE THEME** If you've got access to a bedroom with a mirrored ceiling you'll find the view highly erotic.

# scissors

**HOW TO DO IT** He lies back and she squats over him, facing his feet, and slowly lowers herself onto his erection. She then leans forward and extends her legs behind her, and slowly rocks up and down on his penis.

**WHAT'S RIGHT WITH IT?** Her full weight is bearing down on his penis, creating an incredibly snug fit. She can squeeze his penis with her buttocks during intercourse to make penetration feel even deeper, and can grab onto his legs as she thrusts to help her balance. The more she shifts around, the more different parts of the penis and vagina can be stimulated. If she's worried about putting too much weight on him, she can lean into his thighs.

**WHAT'S WRONG WITH IT?** She can't lie still because the angle of her vagina around his penis would be too uncomfortable for him. And if she's not confident about the way her bottom looks, this isn't the position for her!

**VARIATIONS ON THE THEME** If he's got a foot fetish, this is the perfect position in which to indulge it – he can suck on her toes during their lovemaking.

# female missionary

**HOW TO DO IT** He lies back while she climbs on top of him, facing forwards, supporting her weight on her forearms and extending her legs behind her. She moves her whole body up and down to massage his penis. She can press her legs together to increase clitoral stimulation, or spread them wide for deeper penetration.

**WHAT'S RIGHT WITH IT?** This is one of the only woman-on-top positions where you're close enough to kiss and talk throughout, which creates intimacy. Both of you can enjoy full-body, skin-on-skin contact, and sensitive areas like the breasts are naturally stimulated, while his pubic bone rubs against her clitoris. Stopping the motion for a second to bend down and kiss can delay his orgasm: lovely if you want to keep him from coming too soon.

**WHAT'S WRONG WITH IT?** Although some men love it when women take the lead like this, it can be frustrating not to be able to control the depth and speed of penetration. And if there's a big difference in your heights, this doesn't work.

**VARIATIONS ON THE THEME** This is a fantastic position for him to enjoy if he likes to be restrained during sex. Cuff him to the bedpost, tie his legs down and have your wicked way with him!

**HOW TO DO IT** He lies flat on his back. She squats over him as she would in the reverse rodeo position. But instead of lowering herself up and down on his penis, she gradually leans forwards so that her breasts are touching his legs and extends her legs behind her so that she is lying outstretched on top of him. This needs to be done very slowly: the penis tends to point upwards when it's erect, and as she lowers herself, the vaginal wall will pull it down slightly. Although it seems like an impossible angle in terms of penetration, the walls of the vagina are very elastic and should comfortably accommodate his penis if she takes her time. When she's in position, she then rolls her hips in a gentle figure-of-eight movement to stimulate him.

**WHAT'S RIGHT WITH IT?** A relaxing, low-energy position for men who usually take the lead in bed. If she spreads her legs he can see himself penetrating her from a unique angle. She enjoys the unusual feeling of the soft skin of his balls softly caressing her clitoris.

**WHAT'S WRONG WITH IT?** Younger men, whose erections are firmer and more upright, may experience discomfort.

**VARIATIONS ON THE THEME** He props himself up on a few pillows and holds a video camera to capture the action – this hand-held, erotic home movie style is known as 'gonzo' in the porn industry.

**HOW TO DO IT** He sits up on the bed with his legs slightly bent. She lowers herself onto his erection, wraps her arms around his neck to balance and hooks both of her legs over his shoulders. Orgasm is reached by a slow, rocking motion.

**WHAT'S RIGHT WITH IT?** This position is very intimate: you're quite literally wrapped up in each other and it's easy to talk and kiss throughout. It also combines deep penetration with access to her clitoris, increasing her chances of simultaneous vaginal and clitoral orgasm. As you can't move very much, it's slow, gentle and sensual.

**WHAT'S WRONG WITH IT?** Balancing isn't easy – if you find it hard, try it with him leaning back against the headboard. She'll need to be quite supple to keep her legs in place throughout intercourse. And if you like to thrust vigorously, there's little room to do that here.

**VARIATIONS ON THE THEME** Sex in this position is even steamier if she keeps her stockings and suspenders on throughout – he can kiss and stroke her sexy legs during intercourse.

# man on top

Whoever said man-on-top sex was traditional and boring obviously hasn't tried these highly erotic twists. The following positions are designed to bring out the masculine and feminine qualities in each of you during lovemaking, and are powerful and passionate.

# the tabletop

**HOW TO DO IT** She lies on a flat surface like a table with her legs in the air. He leans against her legs, supporting her and holding her feet together, while he penetrates her.

**WHAT'S RIGHT WITH IT?** Great for when you want to take sex out of the bedroom – this is fab for the kitchen table, your desk at work or the car bonnet. The angle of her vagina in this position stimulates every nerve ending in his penis, from the sensitive head to the shaft. This is also the best man-on-top position for hitting her G-spot. Clitoral stimulation is possible and she can play with her breasts to great effect as she lies on her back.

**WHAT'S WRONG WITH IT?** She might feel a bit vulnerable, and he has to make sure he's holding her at all times so she doesn't go flying off the table – which might put him off his stroke.

**VARIATIONS ON THE THEME** She wears thigh-high leather boots with spiky heels that dig into his shoulders, nearly crossing the fine line between pleasure and pain.

**HOW TO DO IT** She lies on her back with her legs parted. He lies over her, supporting his weight on his elbows, enters her, and thrusts.

**WHAT'S RIGHT WITH IT?** This isn't the most popular lovemaking position for nothing: it's powerfully erotic, with the woman at her most open and vulnerable and the man able to exercise his full sexual power. He controls most of the thrusting and there's very little effort involved for her. Kissing and talking is possible throughout, as is all-important eye contact. There's close body contact too.

**WHAT'S WRONG WITH IT?** It offers little for the woman who wants to take the lead, and it can be hard to maintain clitoral stimulation.

**VARIATIONS ON THE THEME** The chances of her reaching orgasm are much greater if she places a pillow under her hips. This alters the entire tilt of her pelvis, exposing her clitoris to much more friction.

# the flower press

**HOW TO DO IT** He kneels on the bed and she lies back and brings her knees right up to her chin, so that when he enters her, her feet are at either side of his head or resting on his chest. He holds onto her thighs or shins, and she grabs onto his hips.

**WHAT'S RIGHT WITH IT?** Her pelvis really tilts up, allowing for perhaps the deepest penetration possible in a man-on-top position. If he likes feet, this is great. Because the two bodies aren't squashed together her breasts and clitoris can be stimulated. She can also slide her legs in between his legs and gently tug on his balls or press his perineum.

**WHAT'S WRONG WITH IT?** There's not much scope for kissing. Sometimes he can get carried away with the thrusting because it's so deep, but it's a great position for a man with a small penis.

**VARIATIONS ON THE THEME** Lock her feet around his head by placing her ankles in a pair of leg restraints.

# the tie-me-up tango

**HOW TO DO IT** From a kneeling position, she lies on her back with her legs folded under her thighs so her pelvis is elevated. She flings her arms above her head while he lies on top of her.

**WHAT'S RIGHT WITH IT?** This enables really deep thrusting, and his hands are free to explore erogenous zones that aren't always accessible during intercourse, such as her underarms and sides. Her breasts will also be sensitive to stimulation because they're stretched taut, exposing each nerve ending to his touch. This is an excellent position for lesbian lovemaking, with or without a strap-on, because the friction of two sets of breasts brushing against each other is hugely arousing.

**WHAT'S WRONG WITH IT?** She has to be quite flexible to maintain this position for the entire lovemaking session; her knees and thigh muscles may get quite tired. Also, she can't use her hands to control his hips by thrusting, nor can she stimulate his or her genitals. But that helplessness is part of the attraction here.

**VARIATIONS ON THE THEME** Blindfold her to make her surrender even more complete.

**HOW TO DO IT** She lies on her back, with her arms and legs wide open. He crouches over her on all fours and penetrates her; she wraps her arms and legs around his shoulders and back to maintain penetration – she may want to prop her back and pelvis up on pillows to make it more comfortable.

**WHAT'S RIGHT WITH IT?** She can use her legs to force his thighs and buttocks, driving him deeper in. Lots of movement, rocking and thrusting is possible; the constant shifting of positions and angles ensures that his penis receives top-to-toe stimulation – and there's a greater chance than normal of her G-spot being caressed by the tip of his penis. Homosexual male couples can enjoy this position as part of foreplay, kissing and rubbing against each other, or turn it into the main event – the rubbing together of two erect penises, known as 'frottage', can produce an orgasm in itself.

**WHAT'S WRONG WITH IT?** Opportunities for mutual masturbation and stimulation are limited. He may feel that her arms and legs prevent him from thrusting as much as he wants to. He also needs a pretty strong back as it's supporting much of her bodyweight.

**VARIATIONS ON THE THEME** If you enjoy anal play, having sex in this position using butt-plugs or Thai beads will drive you wild.

# missionary, legs inside

**HOW TO DO IT** She lies on her back and spreads her legs so he can penetrate her. Once he's inside, instead of wrapping her legs around his calves, she slides them down onto the bed so they're straight and resting just inside his thighs.

**WHAT'S RIGHT WITH IT?** By squeezing her legs together, she can make her vagina feel longer and snugger, which is useful for accommodating a man with an extremely large penis. The odd super squeeze of her thighs will also stimulate her clitoris and give her a stronger orgasm; if she wants to regain a bit of control she can use her hands to push his buttocks deeper in. She can squeeze him with her pubococcygeal muscle.

**WHAT'S WRONG WITH IT?** She can't move very much.

**VARIATIONS ON THE THEME** If she gets off on the idea of helplessness, pin her arms down by her sides or strap her to the bed using body wrap or a leather harness.

# side by side

Sex in this position is perfect when you want your lovemaking to be slow and sensuous. Many couples enjoy making love side by side as both partners feel equal – neither of you is on top and you share control of pace and penetration. The following positions also require very little effort!

**HOW TO DO IT** The simplest way to reach this position is to roll over on to your sides from a man-on-top position, sustaining penetration as you go. To start from scratch, she will need to lie on her side and part her legs so that he can penetrate her.

**WHAT'S RIGHT WITH IT?** You can speak, kiss and caress – in fact, you need to keep cuddling throughout as, if you let go suddenly, you might fall backwards and apart. The shallow penetration of this position means its great if he's got an oversized penis.

**WHAT'S WRONG WITH IT?** If you like lots of thrusting, rhythmical sex you'll find this side-by-side position too gentle for you. You also run the risk of squashing each other's thighs.

**VARIATIONS ON THE THEME** Cover yourselves in massage oil and slip-slide all over a rubber sheet to make this position even more exciting.

# spoons

**HOW TO DO IT** She lies on her side while he snuggles up behind her. She then draws up her knees a bit and opens her thighs while he tucks his knees behind her, entering her from the rear.

**WHAT'S RIGHT WITH IT?** Sweet and slow, spoons sex is great for sex at the end of the day when you're both feeling lazy. You don't even have to change positions to fall asleep in each other's arms. This is also a chance to really indulge the super-sensitive erogenous zones around the neck, ears and shoulders, whether that's with a massage or nuzzling and kissing. No position better lends itself to him whispering sweet nothings in her ear.

**WHAT'S WRONG WITH IT?** If his penis is small, or one of you is overweight and you can't snuggle as closely as you'd like, penetration can feel a little too shallow for both of you.

**VARIATIONS ON THE THEME** Cuff your legs together to bring a thrilling, dangerous element of bondage into an otherwise safe and intimate position.

# the back flip

**HOW TO DO IT** An advanced version of the spoons position, he lies on his back and penetrates her from behind while she's snuggled on top of his body, facing away from him.

**WHAT'S RIGHT WITH IT?** He's got great access to her breasts and clitoris and this position will make him feel incredibly masculine as he thrusts, supporting her weight. It's also a good position for her if she finds it easier to climax when they're not face-to-face. When she does orgasm, he'll feel the contractions of her anus and perineum because his penis is close to the back wall of her vagina. If she's much taller or lighter than him, this position is ideal.

**WHAT'S WRONG WITH IT?** If she's heavy, neither partner will have much scope for movement and they won't be able to thrust very much – he might need both of his hands for balancing as well. Also, it's not recommended for couples with back problems – physical fitness is an advantage!

**VARIATIONS ON THE THEME** If you're a fan of *al fresco* sex, this position allows you to soak up the sun on your skin while you sin!

# the 'Y'

**HOW TO DO IT** She lies on her side facing him, with one leg in the air and the other on the bed, propping herself up on one arm – her body should look like a huge 'Y' shape. He straddles the lower leg while the lifted leg rests on his shoulder and he penetrates her from the side.

**WHAT'S RIGHT WITH IT?** You both have a great view of each other's face and body. He can see his penis sliding in and out of her vagina and has a clear view of her anus. He can also stimulate her inner thighs. As her legs are so well spread, he can thrust however he wants – from short, sharp strokes to slow, powerful pumps.

**WHAT'S WRONG WITH IT?** Balancing can be tricky – it can also be difficult for him to establish a steady rhythm.

**VARIATIONS ON THE THEME** This makes a great one to video – especially with a handheld camcorder.

# sitting down

Ladies and gentlemen,
please take your seats
for these intimate sex
positions. Sitting down
lends itself to a variety
of outrageous occasions —
and if you make it a regular
part of your lovemaking
routine, you'll have the
strong, toned thighs of
a ski instructor.

# two turtle doves

**HOW TO DO IT** The couple sit facing each other, with their legs crossed or wrapped around each other's backs. They then inch together until he's penetrating her and slowly rock their way to orgasm, scratching each other's backs and massaging each other's fronts all the way through.

**WHAT'S RIGHT WITH IT?** She's bearing down on his penis with all her weight, making for deep and massaging penetration. Being on top, she calls the shots on the pace and depth; he doesn't have to do very much. Because her legs are spread, the skin around her clitoris is stretched thinner and is even more sensitive to his touch. It's also easy for the couple to kiss. This is a great position for lesbians using a double dildo or vibrators on each other.

**WHAT'S WRONG WITH IT?** It can be hard to balance, so don't let go of each other. The man may feel frustrated if she doesn't thrust as hard or as deep as he likes.

**VARIATIONS ON THE THEME** She can reach between his legs – a well-timed squeeze on the scrotum can send him over the edge.

## lap dance

**HOW TO DO IT** He sits on a chair with his legs together. She sits on his lap, and lowers herself backwards onto his penis. Orgasm is achieved through rocking and thrusting.

**WHAT'S RIGHT WITH IT?** His penis is at a great angle to stimulate her G-spot and they can both reach forwards to play with her clitoris or breasts. The lap dance is fun, but if you prefer positions with a greater range of movement, it's very easy to move from this position, without him having to pull out, into the doggy style or another pose that lets you shake it all about!

**WHAT'S WRONG WITH IT?** Success depends on her moving her thighs to control the depth and the thrust of penetration, which can get quite tiring for her.

**VARIATIONS ON THE THEME** Both of you are looking in the same direction, so this position is great if you're both looking at something that turns you on – try it on the sofa in front of a dirty video, or in front of a full-length mirror.

# sitting pretty

**HOW TO DO IT** He sits in a sturdy chair while she straddles him, her knees up, either side of his chest. Holding onto the back of the chair, she pushes away with her feet and moves up and down on his penis while he caresses her.

**WHAT'S RIGHT WITH IT?** This is a fantastic position for quickie sex, as well as being fun and intimate. Her breasts are in a great position for him to take into his mouth while she bounces up and down. He can control the speed of her movements by placing his hands on her waist and gently guiding her.

**WHAT'S WRONG WITH IT?** As she bears down, her bodyweight can feel heavy on his thighs, which can put him off. And she might be concentrating so hard on moving up and down that she can't relax enough to orgasm.

**VARIATIONS ON THE THEME** For ultimate stimulation, she can use her thighs to raise herself up so that only the tip of his penis is inside her vagina. Using her PC muscles to make sure he doesn't fall out, she can then gently swivel her hips from side to side before slowly sliding back down again so that the whole length of his penis is inside her once more.

# the chairman

**HOW TO DO IT** This position requires a chair – ideally an office chair as you can lower it to a level where you can actually touch the floor. He sits back in the chair and relaxes: she assumes the lapdance position (see page 40) but instead of drawing up her legs, she lets them dangle over the sides of the chair, or squeezes them tightly together either side of his thighs. She can then use her legs to lift her body up and gently bounce up and down on his penis. He can thrust upwards too, although his movement is more limited. NB: if you do use an office chair, make sure the brake is on – the last thing you want is for the pair of you to go wheeling across the room at top speed!

**WHAT'S RIGHT WITH IT?** This position is great for circular motions: the bumping and grinding that creates the subtle, constant stimulation she needs on her clitoris. It's also perfect for hugging, kissing and full body contact. This position also accommodates anal sex.

**WHAT'S WRONG WITH IT?** If her legs are quite short then she'll soon get a bit tired, and there's a risk she'll cut off his circulation. If this happens just switch to lapdance mode.

**VARIATIONS ON THE THEME** For an extra kinky twist, she wears nothing but a pair of stilettos. She'll feel glamorous and empowered, and it'll help her feet reach the floor if they're dangling.

# standing

For urgent, passionate, got-to-have-you-now lovemaking, you can't beat sex standing up. It's demanding and passion-packed, and not for everyday intercourse — but what a treat for a special occasion!

## stairway to heaven

**HOW TO DO IT** She stands on the stair in front of him, facing away from him, and he enters her from behind. Once penetration is established, he circles one arm around her stomach and grabs hold of her leg with the other. She then carefully lifts her legs behind her so he's supporting her.

**WHAT'S RIGHT WITH IT?** This ambitious position is great if you're pretending to star in a porn movie – or indeed, if you're actually filming yourselves. It's exhibitionist, sexy and fun. She'll love the feeling of total sexual surrender while he feels dominant and masculine.

**WHAT'S WRONG WITH IT?** It's incredibly physically demanding: he needs to be pretty strong, and she needs to be flexible. Balancing is hard for both of you, and you'll both tire easily. Get around this by indulging in lots of mutual foreplay first, so that you're both on the brink of orgasm before intercourse takes place.

**VARIATIONS ON THE THEME** If fatigue takes over, she can lean forward and place her hands on the floor. This still offers the deep penetration and naughtiness that's the appeal of the Stairway to Heaven, but is a lot less stressful for both of you!

**HOW TO DO IT** This is the perfect position for those moments when you just can't wait to get to the bedroom, and is designed for maximum orgasms in minimum time. She sits on a surface about the same height as his pelvis and wraps her legs around his back. If there's no available kitchen worktop or desk, you can make love up against the wall, but this offers less support for both of you. She pulls her skirt up and pushes her panties to one side while he unzips his flies or drops his trousers.

**WHAT'S RIGHT WITH IT?** The thrill of having a quickie can speed up the female sexual response, meaning she comes in a fraction of the time she would normally take. Her weight is supported by the worktop so all her energy can be put into her sexual performance rather than standing up straight! This also gives him more scope to thrust.

**WHAT'S WRONG WITH IT?** Sometimes women can't produce enough lubrication in time for quickie sex, no matter how turned on they are. Carry a phial of lube with you to avoid this problem.

**VARIATIONS ON THE THEME** Keeping your clothes on is practical as well as sexy. Wear clothes that can easily be pulled to one side rather than whipped off.

## carry on

**HOW TO DO IT** He begins on his knees and asks her to lower herself onto his erection, facing him. As she does, she wraps her legs around his waist and puts her arms around his neck. Then he slowly stands up, shaking her up and down.

**WHAT'S RIGHT WITH IT?** This position reinforces ideas of masculinity and femininity, which will make you both feel sexy. If the two of you can last until you're ready to orgasm, the sensations will be amazing. There's enough full-body contact and friction between you to turn both of you on and speed orgasm along.

**WHAT'S WRONG WITH IT?** It helps if he's very strong – and won't work at all if she's too heavy for him. If you can't handle more than a minute in this position, incorporate it into your foreplay routine or find a surface on which she can balance her feet, such as the edge of the bed or a kitchen worktop.

**VARIATIONS ON THE THEME** Use a gag so no-one can hear your moans of delight!

# the moulin rouge

**HOW TO DO IT** Stand facing each other: he has his back to a wall so he can lean on it for balance. His legs are about a metre apart and slightly bent so she can lower herself down on his erection. His arms are wrapped around her waist to support her and her arms are resting on his shoulders. He bends his knees so she can lower herself onto his penis, then stands up. When penetration feels snug and secure, she sloooowly pulls one leg up and props her foot on his shoulder. Then she eases into the vertical split by sliding her calf as far up his shoulder as she comfortably can, so that her foot is level with her ear.

**WHAT'S RIGHT WITH IT?** This position gets its name because you get a wonderful sense of being a showgirl – and if he's a leg man, he'll be in seventh heaven.

**WHAT'S WRONG WITH IT?** You need to have the suppleness of a professional can-can dancer in the first place. If you can't even touch your toes without feeling muscle twinges, forget it.

**VARIATIONS ON THE THEME** She wears stockings and a suspender belt and asks him to run his hands up and down her leg – thrilling for him as well as her. Take the fantasy even further by pretending she's an old-fashioned Parisian whore – dig out some foreign money to tuck into her stockings and whisper to each other in a fake French accent. Ooh la la!

## twins

**HOW TO DO IT** Both of you stand on the stairs and instead of him carrying your weight, you position yourself so you're facing each other, and your genitals are at exactly the same height. How you do this depends on how tall you both are – if he's very tall, she'll need to be two steps behind him. Varying the steps you stand on can completely transform this experience. For example, if she's taller, it's not such a tight fit: if he's a lot taller then her whole weight is bearing down on his penis, giving a lovely snug fit for both of you.

**WHAT'S RIGHT WITH IT?** Because you're used to your bodies fitting together in a certain way – for example, her face is usually at his chest height during missionary sex – finding that you're suddenly face-to-face and can kiss without craning your necks is a huge turn-on.

**WHAT'S WRONG WITH IT?** Your knees will get very tired quickly. Even though he's not technically bearing her weight, she will inevitably push down on him during lovemaking and he might find it hard to keep his balance.

**VARIATIONS ON THE THEME** Handcuff yourselves to the banisters. You'll need something to hold on to anyway – but it's so much more thrilling if you can't get away!

# sexplosion

Want the kind of sex you see in the movies? The kind of sex where women have multiple orgasms and both of you come at the same time? The good news is that this dream is entirely possible with these advanced techniques. They take a while to master, but once you've got the hang of them, they'll become your new favourite positions!

# the cat

**HOW TO DO IT** Coming together is totally achievable with this incredible position. Short for the Coital Alignment Technique, the cat is a new approach to intercourse based on pressure and rocking motions rather than thrusting. He gets on top of her, lining his pelvis up over hers. His penis is inside, but he's riding high so the base of his penis is just outside her vagina, and his pubic bone is pressing down on her pubic hair. She wraps her legs around his thighs and rests her ankles on his calves. They then move just their pelvises, not their arms or legs, at the same speed, pushing up and down against each other. The aim is to move in the same way at the same speed.

**WHAT'S RIGHT WITH IT?** Not only are women three times more likely to experience orgasm through this technique, but also it delays the male orgasm so your chances of coming together are greater.

**WHAT'S WRONG WITH IT?** The technique is not an easy one to master because it depends on the rocking and rolling mechanism rather than thrusting, which is the way we all learn how to have sex. It does take patience, and can be uncomfortable if she's much smaller than him.

**VARIATIONS ON THE THEME** Play a slow, sexy song that turns both of you on and see if you can keep time to the music.

**HOW TO DO IT** This is the best position for women to achieve multiple orgasms. He lies back while she lowers herself onto him. Then she draws her legs up so her knees are parallel with her chest, and shifts her pelvis so that her clitoris is directly over his pubic bone. Orgasm is reached by gently rocking over him. He should hold off orgasm until hers has been achieved. Then, if she's able to climax again, penetration can continue. If not, she can help him orgasm by masturbating him or performing fellatio.

**WHAT'S RIGHT WITH IT?** This position combines the three factors most likely to contribute to female orgasm: full body contact, clitoral attention and varying degrees of vaginal stimulation. She controls the position of her pelvis so she can be sure that her clitoris is aligned with his pubic bone, and because he can't thrust, she can manipulate the movements to suit her needs. By drawing her legs up towards her chest, she can alter the angle and depth of her vagina, making it much more likely that his penis will stimulate her G-spot.

**WHAT'S WRONG WITH IT?** If the woman wants a multiple orgasm she's going to have to work quite hard for it, and this takes practice and patience to master. But the end will justify the means!

**VARIATIONS ON THE THEME** For a mind-blowing climax for both of you, use a sex toy that combines a cock ring with a clitoral vibrator.

# rear entry

If it's deep penetration and G-spot stimulation you're after, rear-entry sex does it every time. This kind of sex tends to be fast and furious, as many people find it so arousing that they can't contain their climax for more than a couple of minutes. Because the position of the female G-spot isn't the same in every woman, try a few variations on the theme to see what works for you.

**the doggy**

**HOW TO DO IT** She kneels on all fours, her legs slightly parted. He kneels up behind her and penetrates her vagina from behind, holding onto her hips, and thrusts.

**WHAT'S RIGHT WITH IT?** This is the most common rear-entry sex position for lots of good reasons. The angle of penetration means that his penis is in prime position to caress her G-spot, which is located on the front wall of her vagina. For women who know for sure they have a G-spot, this is a firm favourite. For women who aren't sure, this is a fun way to find out – and there's always the option of stroking her own clitoris while he thrusts. Although he ultimately controls penetration, she can move in time with his rhythm, bearing down and backwards on his penis to make the penetration – which is already deep – even more intense. He can enjoy watching his penis enter her vagina.

**WHAT'S WRONG WITH IT?** If his penis is very large, this position can be a little overwhelming. Some women also find it too impersonal and animalistic. Because it's such an intense buzz, many men experience premature ejaculation in this position.

**VARIATIONS ON THE THEME** This position is great for dirty talk – play animal games by putting her on a collar and lead and listen to her yelp with pleasure.

## layers

**HOW TO DO IT** She lies on her front and raises her behind towards him, spreading her legs to make penetration easier for him. He lies on top of her, resting his weight on his elbows, takes her from behind and thrusts backwards and forwards.

**WHAT'S RIGHT WITH IT?** This is great for the man who enjoys being in total control during sex – she can barely move and he's in charge of the depth and pace. By the same token, it's a real turn-on for the woman who loves to surrender during lovemaking. Penetration is snug for him and stimulates her G-spot. Even better, the friction he's causing should mean that her clitoris rubs deliciously against the bedclothes. He can also plant sexy kisses on erogenous zones such as her ears and neck.

**WHAT'S WRONG WITH IT?** If she's top heavy, this might get uncomfortable for her, so slip a pillow or a folded-up towel under her midriff. It's also hard for her to access her clitoris manually.

**VARIATIONS ON THE THEME** This is a great position in which to play spanking games, using a hand, the back of a hairbrush or a custom-made paddle.

# standing doggy

**HOW TO DO IT** He needs a full erection before attempting this position. She stands leaning against a wall or holding onto something for support. He gets behind her and bends his legs until he's low enough to penetrate her from the rear. You'll both have an even greater range of movement if she bends down during this one – she can hold onto his ankles to help her balance.

**WHAT'S RIGHT WITH IT?** It's urgent, animalistic and energetic. Her closed legs act as an extension of the vagina, making for tighter penetration for him and stimulating the nerve endings on her labia and inner thighs. It's great if you like the idea of anal sex but don't want to try it, as it's an unusual sensation and you can't really see what's going on, so you're free to fantasise.

**WHAT'S WRONG WITH IT?** It might be a little too energetic for some. It also doesn't work if there's a big discrepancy in height. This position is perfect, however, for lesbians of about the same height, wearing a strap-on.

**VARIATIONS ON THE THEME** She keeps her fingernails long so she can leave little crescent-shaped imprints when she grabs on to his buttocks, begging to have him deeper inside her.

# the big L

**HOW TO DO IT** She lies on her side with her legs at a ninety-degree angle to her torso, so that from above her body forms an L shape. He kneels on the bed, his hips aligned with hers. If he wants to, he can put his hands on her hips to steady himself. She parts her legs slightly to allow him to penetrate, and then squeezes them together to give his penis a delicious massage as he thrusts in and out of her. It can be hard work keeping her legs clamped together during intercourse – crossing them at the knee or ankle can help her do this without getting cramp!

**WHAT'S RIGHT WITH IT?** This position offers deep penetration for her, and her inner thighs act as an extension of her vagina, making him feel incredibly snug. Even though she can't use her hands to play with her clitoris, some women find that by pressing their legs tightly together, the clitoris becomes engorged and the whole pelvic area becomes even more sensitive.

**WHAT'S WRONG WITH IT?** This position is so delicious he'll want to thrust very vigorously, running the risk of slipping out of her vagina.

**VARIATIONS ON THE THEME** She twists her upper body so that she's lying on her back, but keeps her legs to one side – this way you combine the snug, rear-entry physical sensations of this position with face-to-face contact: kissing is possible, and he can watch while she stimulates her own breasts and belly.

# head rush

**HOW TO DO IT** She lies on her back, her hands propping her weight up as though she's about to do a shoulderstand. He kneels before her and pulls her ankles up towards his shoulders, so her legs are resting on his body and her ankles are around his neck.

**WHAT'S RIGHT WITH IT?** The upside-down position makes the blood rush to her head, which leads to an all-over tingly orgasm. He controls the penetration. The unusual view for both partners means the novelty is thrilling. He can also access her clitoris if he's brave enough to let go of her legs for a second.

**WHAT'S WRONG WITH IT?** The position requires suppleness and stamina on the part of both of you. Penetration can be difficult if you're not used to this position.

**VARIATIONS ON THE THEME** She shaves her pubic hair to make his view even more arousing – or he can shave it for her as a part of their foreplay.

# the wheelbarrow

**HOW TO DO IT** She begins on all fours either on the floor, or a bed. He carefully takes hold of her ankles and raises them to level with his hips, so her hands are the only part of her body on the floor and her pelvis is in mid-air. The man lifts her legs up and holds them spread apart as he penetrates her from behind. The woman can also wrap her legs around the man's waist (crossing her ankles behind her back) for extra support.

**WHAT'S RIGHT WITH IT?** This position gives the man a nice view of his partner's backside, and is good for G-spot stimulation. Her breasts will jiggle about a lot, and even if he can't see it happening, it means that the blood flows to them and her nipples will be ultra-sensitive to the touch if you then decide to swap into a face-to-face position.

**WHAT'S WRONG WITH IT?** It requires upper body strength from both of you. If she has any issues about her body, particularly her ass, she might feel a bit vulnerable and exposed. She has to trust him not to drop her as well – if she's worrying about him bearing her weight, she won't climax.

**VARIATIONS ON THE THEME** If it's too wobbly, try leaning your upper body on a bed or chair rather than trying to support your whole body with your arms. Just make sure she has a pillow placed under her breasts to absorb some of the shock of the vigorous thrusting.

# anal sex

The positions here can be
incorporated into either
heterosexual or homosexual
lovemaking. Homosexual men
enjoy anal sex because the
prostate gland (which nestles
a couple of centimetres or so up
the front wall of the rectum) is
stimulated, occasionally to the
point of orgasm. Women who
enjoy anal sex say they like the
unusual depth and snugness
it provides. Whether you're a

girl–boy couple, a boy–boy couple or even a girl–girl couple using a strap-on, the rules are the same for anal sex: you should always use lubricant, because unlike the vagina, the anus doesn't produce its own natural juices. And, even if you've both been given a clean bill of sexual health, you should always use extra-strong condoms, as anal sex makes both of you more vulnerable to infection.

## bedrock

**HOW TO DO IT** She lies with her back on the edge of the bed and her legs raised. She may need to put a pillow or two under her pelvis for ease of access. He stands on the floor and penetrates her, grabbing onto her legs or thighs, if necessary, to balance.

**WHAT'S RIGHT WITH IT?** Partners can maintain eye contact throughout intercourse, and she can vary the degree of penetration by putting her legs up on his chest to make it deeper, or wrap her legs around his back to increase the feeling of intimacy and involvement. This position offers a good opportunity for vaginal and clitoral stimulation as well.

**WHAT'S WRONG WITH IT?** The thrusting is a lot of work for him, and she can feel as though the lovemaking is out of her control.

**VARIATIONS ON THE THEME** Great for couples into SM and bondage: she can whip him on the buttocks during intercourse with a cat-o'-nine-tails.

# the right angle

**HOW TO DO IT** She leans forward, with her upper body at a right angle to her legs. She supports herself by leaning on a surface, while her partner stands behind and penetrates her from the rear, holding on to her thighs.

**WHAT'S RIGHT WITH IT?** Because her anus is stretched and exposed in this position, penetration is easy and quick. The angle of her rectum also means that penetration is deep and satisfying. Because she's leaning on something, thrusting is easy for him, and so is balancing.

**WHAT'S WRONG WITH IT?** It can feel a little impersonal and out of control for the recipient. Also, penetration is sometimes so deep that the penetrating partner can get a little carried away.

**VARIATIONS ON THE THEME** Lean over a sturdy banister at the top of your stairs for an even giddier sensation.

# the snake

**HOW TO DO IT** She lies on her stomach and spreads her legs while he penetrates her from behind, supporting his bodyweight on his arms. She might need to put a pillow or a cushion under her hips to facilitate penetration.

**WHAT'S RIGHT WITH IT?** Penetration is shallow, so it's ideal if he's got a particularly big penis that she can't accommodate comfortably. There's also highly enjoyable friction on the stomachs and nipples of both partners, and the rubbing of the clitoris against the bed for her (or the penis of the penetrated partner during gay sex).

**WHAT'S WRONG WITH IT?** See above – it can result in less sensation for the guy. The woman will find it hard to reach her clitoris or, if the sex is between homosexual men, the recipient won't easily be able to stimulate his penis manually.

**VARIATIONS ON THE THEME** Do it in front of a mirror so you can see each other's face and talk to each other while you make love.

# the jigsaw

**HOW TO DO IT** She lies on her side and draws her knees up to her chest. He nuzzles into her back and takes her from behind.

**WHAT'S RIGHT WITH IT?** She can masturbate herself, or he can play with her clitoris and breasts, while she can clench her buttocks to massage the base of his penis. It's also very intimate and nurturing – he can hold her and whisper in her ear. Two men in this position will both have access to the penis of the penetrated partner and be able to caress his balls.

**WHAT'S WRONG WITH IT?** It can be hard for him to build up a good deep thrust, and he might crush his partner's thighs. Movement can be restricted for both of you and you might lose a little of the delicious friction that helps you both reach orgasm. Get round this by wearing a ribbed condom that will enhance sensation.

**VARIATIONS ON THE THEME** If she pulls her legs in towards her chest, she will shorten the rectal passage, making penetration shallower. Or why not try doing the Jigsaw in front of a mirror for even greater intimacy?

# simultaneous oral sex positions

The 69 – in which you both give each other oral sex at the same time – is a classic sex position even though no penetration is involved, and it's a great favourite with homosexual and heterosexual couples alike. It's not easy to both give and receive oral sex at the same time, so don't worry if you don't see stars the first time you do it. The 69 is great for those times when you're feeling fun and frisky and orgasm isn't the immediate goal, or save it for occasions when you're both so horny that the lightest touch will bring you to orgasm.

**HOW TO DO IT** Her on top: he lies flat on his back with his arms by his sides or around her buttocks. She's on all fours with her bottom in the air, hovering over his face. She rests on her forearms, her mouth poised over his penis. The benefits of this position are that she can control the rhythm of the cunnilingus she's receiving by rocking her hips in time and she's perfectly positioned to pay attention to every inch of his penis. Her breasts will brush against his belly and thighs, which will turn him on and the friction on her nipples will stimulate her, too.

**WHAT'S RIGHT WITH IT?** This is the most common 69 position for the simple reason that women tend to be lighter than men. And of course, from his point of view, there's less work for his pleasure! His arms are free to caress her or to stimulate himself if she gets tired.

**WHAT'S WRONG WITH IT?** Because it's hard to concentrate on giving head and getting it at the same time, you need to take it in turns. Spend alternate minutes stimulating one another's genitals – this should build up to a tremendous orgasm for both of you. Or use it as foreplay and savour what you've just done while you're making love in a more conventional position.

**VARIATIONS ON THE THEME** Sucking on each other's toes clearly requires impeccable foot hygiene but it's a surprisingly enjoyable and overwhelmingly intimate feeling – which is just the soft sensation you need during this physically demanding, hot and horny position.

## 69 — man on top

**HOW TO DO IT** She lies back on the bed, legs slightly parted, arms by her side. He crouches over her on all fours and is in an excellent position to play with her breasts. This is a comfortable position for him because his neck won't start to ache. He can also use her inner thighs as a pillow.

**WHAT'S RIGHT WITH IT?** He can see exactly what he's doing so there's no excuse for him not finding her clitoris and paying it lots of attention with his tongue.

**WHAT'S WRONG WITH IT?** It's not easy for the woman to take him fully into her mouth from this angle, but he can thrust against her neck, cheeks and breasts and she's free to use her tongue on his anus, balls and perineum (the super-sensitive piece of skin between his balls and anus).

**VARIATIONS ON THE THEME** If she spreads her legs as wide as she can, the skin surrounding the clitoris and vagina will be stretched tight, leaving it more exposed and sensitive, and giving him a unique close-up look at her genitals. He can also pay attention to the inner thighs, an often-neglected erogenous zone.

# kama sutra

The Ancient Indians used sex as a way of achieving spiritual closeness, worshipping the gods and cleansing the soul – and who are we to argue with that? In the 4th Century BC, one Prince Vatsyayana became the world's first sexpert when he wrote the *Kama Sutra*, a manual of sex positions designed to emphasise communication rather than orgasm, and these positions are designed to delay the man's climax and intensify the woman's. The *Kama Sutra* teaches that the mind and spirit are the biggest erogenous zones of all, so before attempting lovemaking in these positions, lie side by side and synchronise your breathing until you're both breathing in the same rhythm – this helps you tune into each other's bodies. And turn your bedroom into an oasis of calm and tranquillity – in the *Kama Sutra*, Vatsyayana recommends the bed is 'covered with a white cloth and strewn with flowers and garlands.'

## the yab-yum

**HOW TO DO IT** Begin as though you were making love in the two turtle doves position (see page 38) but instead of thrusting up and down, the woman clenches and unclenches her vaginal muscles, keeping up just enough pelvic movement to keep his penis erect inside her, but not so much that he feels he's approaching climax. If he's becoming overstimulated she can raise her legs over his shoulders. This offers her the deeper penetration she needs, while the top of her vagina is stretched and lengthened by this position, denying him the stimulation at the tip of the penis that might trip him over into premature climax.

**WHAT'S RIGHT WITH IT?** Tantric practioners believe that if a man's spine is erect during intercourse, he's able to moderate his passion and delay his ejaculation for up to six hours (although that might be a little ambitious for those of us not schooled in the discipline). It's true that he's not likely to climax too soon, and this is a fabulous position for letting him focus not on his own pleasure but on that of his partner.

**WHAT'S WRONG WITH IT?** As with all tantric positions, the yab-yum offers the temptation to abandon the soft, subtle movements for traditional, in-out, in-out thrusting. Resist it!

**VARIATIONS ON THE THEME** When you've both reached orgasm, don't pull apart: satisfied, remain in the yab-yum position, breathing harmoniously until his penis is totally limp. We rarely allow this to happen, but it's a very gentle, intimate end to a lovemaking session.

# widely opened position

**HOW TO DO IT** Begin as though you were making love in the missionary position: he's on top, resting on his elbows, she's lying on her back. Once he's snugly inside her, she wraps her legs around his back, raising her pelvis as she does so, ensuring that her clitoris remains in contact with his pubic bone. He then rises up on all fours, so that he is bearing her whole bodyweight with his back and shoulders. He stays absolutely stationary while she rubs her clitoris against his pubic bone, making sure she gets the stimulation she needs to orgasm, which giving him just enough friction to maintain his erection, but not quite enough to cause him to climax.

**WHAT'S RIGHT WITH IT?** It's good for chaps who suffer from premature ejaculation: the effort it takes him to carry her bodyweight can buy precious extra minutes of intercourse as blood rushes away from his erection to his upper body muscles.

**WHAT'S WRONG WITH IT?** The widely opened position obviously depends on a reasonably light woman and a reasonably strong man who doesn't have any back problems. Although this position gives her clitoris full exposure to the friction of intercourse he may miss the feeling of tight containment he gets when she closes her legs against his penis.

**VARIATIONS ON THE THEME** As she approaches orgasm, she can afford to arouse him a little more. If she pulls herself only halfway onto his penis, she focuses on the nerve endings in the super-sensitive tip of his penis.

# the second posture
# of the perfumed garden

**HOW TO DO IT** Begin as with missionary but instead of lying with her legs on the bed, she bends them back so that her knees are touching her chest and her legs are outstretched, slightly parted so he can bend down and kiss her. He needs to use his hands to support his weight: she can grip her ankles to steady her legs and allow him to enter her more easily.

**WHAT'S RIGHT WITH IT?** The Kama Sutra recommends this for a man with a very short penis. As you might expect, this allows the deepest penetration of all.

**WHAT'S WRONG WITH IT?** She may find vaginal thrusting too painful and stimulating – especially if his penis is larger than usual – and need him to back off a little if he gets too excited.

**VARIATIONS ON THE THEME** Slipping on a vibrating cock ring should give her the clitoral stimulation she needs to make this an intense but enjoyable position for both of you.

**HOW TO DO IT** Think of it as the missionary position, but the man has spun round: that's where it gets its name from. The very ambitious might be tempted to start off in male missionary position and then turn round like a corkscrew, but I would advise against this for all but the most advanced Tantra practitioners. Instead, she lies on her back with her legs slightly apart, while he lies on top of her, facing her feet. His torso is between her legs while his arms are either side of her legs and his legs either side of her shoulders. Penetration is almost impossible unless she tilts her pelvis upwards to accommodate his penis: if she puts a couple of pillows underneath her hips it will be much easier.

The shallow depth means that you use a gentle rocking motion rather than the vigorous thrusting you can get away with in other positions.

**WHAT'S RIGHT WITH IT?** He can't penetrate her very deeply, so his ultra-sensitive tip of his penis gets lots of attention. She will enjoy the feeling of his balls caressing her vagina.

**WHAT'S WRONG WITH IT?** Even if he wants to thrust, the angle will be too uncomfortable to allow this. And it's hard to keep the synchronised breathing and eye contact that makes Kama Sutra sex so special when your heads are at opposite ends of the bed.

**VARIATIONS ON THE THEME** You'll be seeing each other's feet at quite close range – an eyeful of hard skin and corns is nobody's idea of an aphrodisiac. Soak in the bath together beforehand and use a foot scrub and lotion to give each other a pampering pedicure beforehand.

# advanced lovers only

For the very bold only….

# the mexican wave

**HOW TO DO IT** She lies back on the bed with her legs up in the air, wide open. He's facing away from her and arranges himself so he's on all fours. He then hooks his legs over her hips so that his feet are either side of her shoulders, and when he's secure in that position, he gradually eases his penis inside her. She rests her legs on his back and plays with his balls as he thrusts back and forth.

**WHAT'S RIGHT WITH IT?** You're only really touching using your legs and genitals (as opposed to arms, legs and fronts and all the places that are usually stimulated during intercourse); because all the stimulation is concentrated in the lower body, the sensations there are more intense than usual.

**WHAT'S WRONG WITH IT?** Your heads are as far away as they can be so if you want to talk dirty, you're gonna have to shout so loud you wake the neighbours. And kissing's out of the question.

**VARIATIONS ON THE THEME** She holds onto his hips and pulls herself up so as to intensify the sensations even further.

## topsy-pervy

**HOW TO DO IT** He lies down with his knees curled up to his chest. She straddles him with his legs under her arms to steady her, and her legs either side of his body. She lowers herself until he's deep inside her and moves up and down in a pumping action, controlling the depth and motion of the thrusts.

**WHAT'S RIGHT WITH IT?** You both get a great view and this position allows good access to the sensitive walls of her vagina. She can show her dominant side while he lies submissive.

**WHAT'S WRONG WITH IT?** Her arms are keeping her balanced so she can't use them to stimulate him, or to help herself reach orgasm. You both need pretty sturdy thigh muscles.

**VARIATIONS ON THE THEME** As both of you are so busy balancing, your all-important clitoral stimulation might get bypassed, so take the hands-free option with a tiny clitoral vibrator that straps to her like a pair of vibrating knickers or a small strap-on stimulator especially designed for the clitoris.

# the knee-trembler

**HOW TO DO IT** Both kneel on the stairs facing upwards: she's on the step above him. She sits back onto his lap while he holds her hips and thrusts from behind. You can both move up and down in a slow, steady rhythm, using your thigh muscles and that will increase blood flow to those areas, making orgasm more intense.

**WHAT'S RIGHT WITH IT?** This position gives him deep access combined with more of a grinding motion than the usual from-behind fast thrusting. Sometimes rear-entry sex can be a bit overwhelming for her: in this position, she can relax and enjoy the sensation, as well as stimulate her clitoris.

**WHAT'S WRONG WITH IT?** You can't kiss face-to-face, although he can kiss the back of her neck. It's possible that cramp will set in before orgasmic bliss!

**VARIATIONS ON THE THEME**
As you're both facing the same way, why not watch an erotic video together? Or he can read an erotic novel over her shoulder. His breath on her neck and voice in her ear will drive her wild.

## head over heels

**HOW TO DO IT** She lies stomach down on the bed, with her head, arms and shoulders dangling over the edge of the bed and her hands placed palm-downwards on the floor. He slides behind her so that his body is positioned directly over hers and his hands are either beside or directly behind hers and the front of his torso is pressed into her back. His head is also hanging over the edge of the bed. Then he penetrates her and slides in and out. Start slowly to see if you like the way this feels and to make sure you've got your balance before building up to more vigorous thrusts.

**WHAT'S RIGHT WITH IT?** Because you've got a rush of blood – and therefore oxygen – to your head, your orgasm will invigorate your mind and make your head spin as well as your body.

**WHAT'S WRONG WITH IT?** Again, you might get dizzy before you get horny, so avoid this one if you suffer from vertigo or blackouts. The position won't work unless his arms are longer than hers.

**VARIATIONS ON THE THEME** If she slides a pillow underneath her waist, it will tilt the angle of her hips so that his penis is more likely to brush against her G-spot on the front wall of her vagina. Plus, if she's busty, it'll stop her breasts feeling squashed underneath his weight.

cat on a hot tin roof

**HOW TO DO IT** He sits in a comfortable armchair or a sofa. She sits on his lap, facing away from him, and slowly tilts her body forward until her face is between his knees and her bottom and genitals are raised up towards his face. Her legs are either side of his, either squatting or kneeling, whichever is more comfortable for her. She then gently lowers herself down onto his erection and slowly works her way up and down, keeping her ass up in the air.

**WHAT'S RIGHT WITH IT?** It's a visual treat beyond imagination for men who really like looking at and playing with her ass during sex: even better for girls who like having a finger inserted into their anus during sex.

**WHAT'S WRONG WITH IT?** Some women will feel vulnerable and exposed – if he isn't into anal play, it will turn him off, too. The workload is rather uneven. She has to put a lot of effort in, while he just sits there and enjoys the show (not that he'll complain).

**VARIATIONS ON THE THEME** Instead of stimulating her anus with a finger, he can use his tongue to tease and probe. This is known as 'rimming' in gay circles, and devotees say it's an amazing sensation. It goes without saying she should be fresh from the shower before he attempts this.

## the rocking horse

**HOW TO DO IT** She lies on the bed or floor on her stomach, resting on her elbows. Her legs are straight and slightly apart. He sits behind her buttocks with his legs in front of him and his hands on either side of her body for support. He leans back at a 45-degree angle to her body so he can join his genitals with hers and rocks back and forth.

**WHAT'S RIGHT WITH IT?** He's totally in control, and her sense of thrilling vulnerability is heightened by the fact she can't see what he's doing, and doesn't know when the next stroke is coming. Plus the feeling of his pelvic bone rubbing her bottom and his balls slapping against her inner thighs is a novel sensation.

**WHAT'S WRONG WITH IT?** If she wants any stimulation on her clitoris, she's going to have to do it herself and it won't be easy to slide her hand forward and underneath her body to reach her clitoris, as she's bearing not only her weight but his.

**VARIATIONS ON THE THEME** She can experiment with parting her legs so he can see his penis sliding in and out of her, or squeezing them together for a tight fit that both of you will love.